A Sure and Certain Hope
(My Life in Verse)

Kevin Hope

Presentation by *BookLeaf Publishing*

Web: www.bookleafpub.com

E-mail: info@bookleafpub.com

ISBN: 978-93-95255-31-8

First edition 2022

DEDICATION

For my wife, Hazel and my children, Rachael and Adam; and for all those who are explicitly or implicitly mentioned within, past and present. You have all touched my heart to a greater or lesser extent.

ACKNOWLEDGEMENT

This collection of poems was written for the Emily Dickinson challenge established by Bookleaf Publishing. But without my daughter's initial suggestion and reassurance, I might not have taken part.

Rachael, you introduced me to the idea of entering the competition and you kindly read each of the verses, rhymes, sonnets and poems as I wrote them. You gave me valuable feedback as well as your constant encouragement and support throughout the process; and you showed your own creativity in proposing the opening composition. Thank you, my precious girl.

PREFACE

Over the years, I've written numerous rhymes, but never considered them to be poems. For me, they were merely a way, for example, to express good wishes in a more creative way in a greetings card, or a novel way to pass on information by having rhyming words at the end of sentences. But I didn't see myself as a poet!

One definition of a poet suggests "a person who has the gift of poetic thought, imagination, and creation, together with eloquence of expression" and I'm not sure that's me. But then another proposes, simply, that it is a maker of verses, and I can identify with that.

If a poem is a piece of writing in which the expression of feelings and ideas is given intensity by particular attention to diction, sometimes involving rhyme, rhythm, and imagery, then I might just have hit the brief in this short selection.

Getting started was the hard part, but once I had decided on 'my life in verse', the thoughts and ideas started flowing.

I tried to challenge myself to encompass a variety of styles that I just hadn't previously thought about using before, so you can expect a beginners attempt at a sonnet, an acrostic poem, a haiku, non-rhyming stanzas (which didn't come naturally at all!) and alliterative verse.

Reliving my life was hugely satisfying yet extremely moving. The happier times raised a smile and whilst reflecting on the more difficult episodes was painful, it was equally therapeutic.

I hope you enjoy reading about 'my journey' as much as I did writing about it.

Being 64

When I'm 64, wrote John and Paul,
you will still be my Valentine.
We will stay up late drinking wine,
celebrating all that life has to offer.

Our children will have children
and we will rent a cottage and holiday by the sea.

I'll fix the garden
while you knit by the fire.

Well, here I am; at 64,
doing everything they promised, and more.
Older and greyer, but still full of life.
I have grandchildren by my side
reminding me
of the wonderful world in which we live
and keeping me young. At 64

So I present to you a treasury; 'my life in verse',
giving a flavour of the joy,
sorrow and abundance of love
that has been my life so far.

And as I reflect on these many years past
I also look forward in eager anticipation
to what has yet to come. After 64!

Starting out

My early years, as I fondly recall, seemed happy,
relaxed and stress-free;
in those halcyon days in my Lancashire home,
I thought the world revolved around me.
A loving Mum, a caring Dad; I had uncles and
aunties galore,
with a Nanna and Grandad that I loved to the moon;
I couldn't have wanted for more.
And then my baby brother arrived, which was a
bonus I didn't suspect;
it was as though something clicked,
became complete;
our family group made perfect.

My life had a structure, or schedule I guess, about
how it was all to be spent;
it's as though all was planned – the year, months and
weeks, and here's how I recall that it went.
Each Saturday morning we'd be on the bus to Mum's
Mum and Dad's for the day,
we'd weave in and out of the market stalls and stop in
the park for a play.
On Sundays, roles reversed,
they'd catch the bus back,
with my Godmother also in tow.
We'd watch the big films, hear the big hits, talk and
laugh until they had to go.

Then every bank holiday we'd take a trip, and the
format was like Groundhog Day;
same places for drinks, lunches and walks; same café
where we'd stop on the way.
And I remember summer holidays with such
fondness – they never varied over the years,
spending time on the beach, in the sea, in the park;
and running the length of the piers.
We stayed with the same boarding house couple – my
holiday grandparents besides.
We had theatre shows, circus treats in the Tower and,
one day a week, funfair rides!

And, Christmas was such a treat for us all – much the
same, I guess, as anyone;
but the highlight, after Father Christmas of course,
was the family rounds to be done.
We'd set off with Dad, and call for a drink at as many
kinsfolks' houses as we were able
before getting home to where Mum would be serving
up Christmas lunch at the table.

So many memories, I was blessed as a child and it
made me the man I became.
So much has changed now, and not all for the better;
but in my mind it all stays the same.

God Bless The Boys' Brigade

"We have an anchor" the Life Boy said,
sure and stedfast is the plan;
growing in wisdom and stature
and in favour with God and man.
Being part of a global family
that stretches across the world:
with united voice – "my anchor will hold"
as I fly the standard, unfurled.
That Life Boy from so long ago,
through Junior and Company ranks
looks back at all the influences
with affection, recognition and thanks.
The teachings and behaviours adopted,
and the strong foundations they laid,
have helped forge the man who you see today;
so I say "God bless The Boys' Brigade."

Steam Train (to School)

5

School bag in hand
Term starts today
Excited about catching the train
All aboard calls the guard
Main line service pulls away

Thunder through the tunnel
Roar into the daylight
Approach the station
Inhale the strong smell of coal and oil
Navigate the overbridge and so to school

The Bully

What did I do to deserve this?
What did I do that was wrong?
Why did it start in the first place?
Why did it go on so long?
Why didn't anyone notice?
Why didn't anyone care?
What made me weak and submissive?
What made me not want to dare
to stand up for myself in the hallway
or protect myself in the gym?
Why did I hide in the playground,
afraid that I'd be found out by him?
His actions were aggressive but simple.
My punishment? To feel his pain.
He'd catch me alone and make me feel small
and he'd do it again and again.
Who could I turn to to help me?
Who could I talk to and tell
about the anguish, humiliation and hurtful
thoughts I was thinking inside my shell?
Why anyone should be bullied
just makes me very confused:
No one should be demeaned or derided,
no one should be so abused.

So what would I say to my cowardly self,
now that I'm wiser and older?

Easier said than done, I'm quite sure,
"Stand your ground, be brave and be bolder.
You are strong and you matter, so trust me;
have faith in yourself; believe fully!
Speak up and speak out, 'cos you're worthy."
Which is more than I'd say for the bully.

The Smell of the Greasepaint

Treading the boards, amateur style;
I've been known to do it once in a while.
I started quite young, when I first joined a troupe
and I remember my only two words - "Mr Toop."
A line from Pools Paradise – a choirboy I played,
three nights came and went, but the interest stayed.
I enjoyed numerous appearances, too many to list,
but I'll name you my favourites, so you get the gist.
Farces like Wild Goose Chase and Dry Rot,
Panic Stations and One for the Pot.
Comedies – Dear Charles (full of trouble and strife),
and the wonderful Happiest Days of your Life.
Seeing productions from beginning to end,
two nights a week, at least, I would spend
building the set, each time brand new,
painting it, sourcing the furniture too.
Learning lines, not as simple as it seems:
following direction, staging the scenes.

Thank the Lord – dress rehearsal survived
and at long last the opening night has arrived.
Applying the greasepaint – nine and five,
onto the stage, audience there – come alive!
Act 1, 2 and 3, then the blackout falls,
and there's just time left for the curtain calls.
The applause floods the hall, the audience cheer.
Let's do it all again this time next year!

Every step of the way

Not everyone gets a revelation
when the Spirit lands within:
it can be a quiet experience
when those feelings start to begin
to grow and flood your senses,
and you just know that something's occurred,
and that's the way it was with me
when I first really heard His Word.
A Christian retreat in Barnston,
He the potter, I the clay;
I remember how the fire started to burn
like it was only yesterday.
The strength of my faith has peaked and troughed,
but it's only fair to say
that His presence has been felt when I needed it most,
and all it took was to pray.
I've borrowed His might
in the most challenging times,
and I've thanked Him when things were right.
I know I don't give enough attention to Him,
yet He's the Way and the Truth and the Light.
From that teenage epiphany on the Wirral,
right up to the present day
He's been with me, whether I acknowledged it or not,
every step of the way.

Thank You Headmaster

I'd like to thank my Headmaster,
for his timely intervention;
he was instrumental in directing my life
even though that was not his intention!
Now I wasn't academically minded,
which is something I just couldn't hide;
so when I collected my O-Level results
he found me and took me aside.
"Mr Hope", he announced, "5 out of 7's not great
and it pains me, but I must confess
that maybe it's not worth returning next term;
perhaps you should re-assess."
"What do you think you might do?" he inquired.
"What could you do for employ"?
Without thinking, "I'll work in a bank" I replied.
To which he said, "Oh my dear boy
you'll need higher qualifications
than the paltry few that you've got."
I said, "Thank you, Headmaster, I hear what you say
but I think I'll still give it a shot."
And so I applied – still not knowing why
and the rest is just history they say.
It changed the course of my life for the good
and it's brought me to where I am today.
So once again, thank you Headmaster;
without your unwitting correction,
who knows where I'd be; I may not be me
if I'd taken a different direction.

Life and Death

Experiencing the passing of someone close is like a
crushing blow, and each loss brings with it a cocktail
of emotions affecting every part of your being.
I remember my first crushing blow and it makes me
wonder how many crushing blows it would take
before we break?
I never knew my Dad's parents, but one of his older
sisters did everything for me that his Mum would
have done – then she was gone.
I was such a young lad when she was taken too soon;
I didn't appreciate at the time the hole she left, never
to be replaced; what a waste.
My second crushing blow came as a young man
when my Grandad left me; such a quiet giant among
men and I worshipped the ground he walked on.
His illness was a long and a difficult one; then he had
a stroke, and never woke.
I've lost family members along the way and whilst
saying goodbye is never easy, I can't say these
bereavements fitted into the crushing blow category;
but fate and nature hadn't finished with me yet, I
regret.
The crushing blow when my Dad passed away
seemed more intense somehow: the bond, the
closeness, the love.
Over two slow years he suffered and became a
shadow of his former self, and when the time came,
as painful as it was for those left behind, it was a
blessèd release; he was at peace.

My Nanna had been indomitable; a constant
unwavering force: and the crushing blow I felt when
she went was in part watching a frail and fragile old
lady fade away, which belies the woman she had
been.
She'd been full of belief and self-will; so that's how I
remember her still.
There's a natural order to life and it's a crushing blow
when that is defied. How do you reconcile with a
teenager's passing? Didn't seem real; such a raw
deal.
My Godmother was an instrumental figure from my
earliest days and never a week went by without her
presence in my life. For her to be here today and gone
tomorrow was a crushing blow: such was the rapidity
of her illness.
Blue was her colour; the world became duller.

And so to the latest of my crushing blows, and the most recent as well – my lovely Mum.
Someone who bore me, nurtured me, cared for me, loved me. Someone I thought would be around forever – but can't be; won't be; isn't.
The void her leaving created brought with it a hollowness, an emptiness. It'll never be the same again, but although we're apart I've got a piece of her heart.
Death, it seems, is life. How ironic is that?

Home Study

A young man decided to study,
but downed a bottle or two with a buddy.
Being drunk was a factor;
he tried stealing a tractor
but was stopped by a Police fuddy-duddy!

Sometimes

15

Sometimes it can start quite small.
Sometimes it can grow quickly, sometimes
smouldering slowly over time.
Sometimes it can be quite selective.
Sometimes it can be shallow, sometimes deep.
Sometimes it can be rewarding.
Sometimes it can be a blessing, sometimes a curse.
Sometimes it can be life-affirming.
Sometimes it can be strengthening, sometimes
exhausting.
Sometimes it can be treasured.
Sometimes it can last a lifetime, sometimes over in a
heartbeat.
Sometimes it can be all you need.
FRIENDSHIP.

Hazel

Strolling along in the evening, just ambling on down
the street,
never in a month of Sundays did I expect to meet
the woman I'd call my true love, the one on whom
I'd depend;
the one I'd call my soulmate and with whom my
whole life I would spend.
Some people get hit by an arrow; fired by Cupid they
say.
I got struck with a badminton racket; the result was
the same anyway!
Head over heels in a fortnight, engaged within the
year:
a long-distance relationship followed, then wedding
bells rang loud and clear.
All that seems like a lifetime ago, when as
newly-weds we started to build our future together;

and where are we now?
Happy and strong and fulfilled.

First-time Parent

No one can prepare you for the joy
when you first of all lay your sight
on your new-born baby – girl or boy;
a moment of untold delight.
Your elation is tempered with fear though;
will I be up to it all?
The responsible adult, apropos
someone who is just so small.
You cuddle and hold them so gently;
you don't want to be apart.
You listen and watch them intently
and love them with all your heart.
A rollercoaster of emotion.
That sums up parental devotion.

Being a Dad

If I knew then what I know now
about being a responsible Dad,
would it be different, better or worse
than the 30 odd years that I've had?
From holding them close for the first time,
marvelling them feed at the breast,
watching them take those first faltering steps
to seeing them flying the nest;
such a rollercoaster of emotions
and of course it doesn't stop then;
will they be happy, will they be safe,
will there come the time when
they find their own love for their lifetime,
a house, a job or career?
Will they have children to cherish,
will they live far away or be near?
All these conundrums and questions,
all of the hopes, doubts and fears;
good choices, bad ones, the rights and the wrongs,
I've lived them out over the years.
Instilling those family values,
always trying to do what is best.
Luck's played a part, I'm certain of that,
and for what I have now, I feel blessed.
So back to the question I began with,
and if self-indulgence is allowed;
as a Father, a Husband, and now Grandad
I simply could not be more proud.

Moving House

Absolute anarchy abounds inside
Boxes bulging all around
Children crying "I don't want to go"
Dad's diplomacy disappears
Emptiness echoes through the house
Footsteps falling flat
"Goodness gracious, go steady"
Heavy-handed henchmen warned
Imagining images of china
Jingle-jangling, emptied from
Kitchen cupboards, clattering, broken on the floor
Lorry loading; little by little
Moving mountains a box at a time
Nosey neighbours dropping by
Overtly opportunistic!
Prying parasites
Quizzically questioning, "are you leaving that?"
Rooms ready for cleaning
Sweep, scrub, scour
Time to take our leave
Unspoken upset unwittingly revealed
Voicing views through moody silence
Wanderers, wending our way to where
X marks the spot
Your Yale key opens your new front door
Zing zapped, zonk out; welcome home.

Guilt

Invasive maggot, burrowing, reminding.
Relentlessly pulsating.
Omnipresent. Mine.

Vocation

Not everyone gets to do a job
that's rewarding, they excel at, and love;
but when everything comes together,
it fits like a hand in a glove.
It becomes more like a vocation;
a profession to which you were called.
And when I moved into a learning career,
that's when I became enthralled
at the potential that lay before me,
my senses were heightened and stirred;
and the line between working to live
and living to work became blurred.
It certainly wasn't plain sailing;
sacrifices had to be made.
It was only the people around me
and the love and support they displayed
that allowed me to shine, be successful;
without them, I'd be nothing at all.
It's only what they had to surrender
that enabled me to walk tall.

45 Years Later

1974 - hired (by a large finance house)
1979 - inquired (about a London role)
1980 – wired (to be living in the capital)
1983 - desired (to be moved back up north)
1989 - aspired (to a manager's job)
1995 - inspired (by a career change)
2002 - tired (of the politics game)
2005 – acquired (by a quiet, small firm)
2014 – admired (for the work I produced)
2019 – retired (after 45 years)

The Tourist

Ridden, driven, sailed away, flown.
Wife, family, friends, alone.
Asia, Australia, Europe, U.S.
U.A.E., Caribbean Islands no less.
Fortunate, charmed, grateful – even so
there are yet still many more places to go.

Mid-Summer

If I had been born back in the Victorian age,
likely I'd have died before middle age.
As the 20th century dawned, I vow
they'd say I was in the autumn of my years by now.
But having been born in '57, I appraise
I'm only just now in my midsummer days.

The Grandchild Effect

They started out so very tiny,
dependent in every aspect.
I'll gladly do anything for them.
That's the Grandchild effect.

Who knew when it comes to changing nappies,
I'd become so proficient; as well as perfect
at wiping noses and messes.
All part of the Grandchild effect.

Babies not long, two at school now!
And selfishly I want to protect
them from growing up way too soon.
It's called the Grandchild effect.

Their mischief can get them in trouble.
Sometimes what they hear, they select.
The havoc, the mayhem, the mess - all that's fine,
such is the Grandchild effect.

They look so angelic, like cherubs,
yet in my armour, chinks they detect.
But I'm happy to be wrapped round their fingers.
That, for sure, is the Grandchild effect.

We frequently go on an outing,
across zoos, parks and farms we have trekked.
Spending more than intended in gift shops.
What the heck! It's the Grandchild effect.

"Follow us, Grandad" they shout in soft play
and some gaps are so small - should have checked!
But I follow and manage to squeeze through
somehow,
buoyed by the Grandchild effect.

Reading stories becomes an adventure,
with their orders, they like to direct.
"Not like that, Grandad," "louder," "softer," "once
more."
It's allowed with the Grandchild effect.

Sometimes they can run me quite ragged,
but how can I possibly reject
their calls of "again" and "again, Grandad,"
energised by the Grandchild effect.

When I'm not with them, I miss them.
It's disheartening in every respect.
I long for the time when I see them again
to enjoy their Grandchild effect.

They're growing up year after year, of course,
and there will come a time I suspect
they'll have different needs to those they have now:
but they'll still have that Grandchild effect.